a

coach

heading

towards

the

provinces

a
coach
heading
towards
the
provinces

Xifeng Yedu

translated by Ouyang Yu

PUNCHER & WATTMANN

First published in 2022
Published by Puncher and Wattmann
PO Box 279
Waratah NSW 2298

http://www.puncherandwattmann.com
puncherandwattmann@bigpond.com

ISBN   9781922571199

Cover design by Miranda Douglas
Typesetting by Morgan Arnett
Printed by Lightning Source International

A catalogue record for this
book is available from the
National Library of Australia

Contents

爱四样

我喜欢郊外翻滚的麦浪
如果土地不曾被污染
更远的郊外，就一定还有清澈的溪流
我喜欢万米之上机舱外的天空
阴霾尽扫，世界大同
我喜欢做梦，白日梦、梦中梦
我在梦里写诗、打铁、为国旗漆上新色
当然我最喜欢的还是女人，我时刻攥一把
稀薄的爱情，伺机塞进她们的贴身衣袋
然后让她们附体我的充气娃娃
我尤其喜欢水性杨花那类
喜欢她们在风中飘
迎着故乡和春天的味道

Four Things I Love

I love the rolling waves of wheat outside the city
If the earth is not polluted
There must be clean creeks further outside the city
I love the skies outside the plane 10000 metres above the earth
Where the smog is swept clean and Greater Harmony exists
I love dreaming, daydreaming, dreamdreaming
In which I write poetry, forge iron and paint the national flag with a new colour
But, of course, I love women best and I always grip a handful
Of thin love, putting it inside the pocket close to their bodies on the off chance
And getting them embodied in my inflatable doll
I particularly love the kind of watery nature
The way they drift in the air, like the polar flowers
Towards the smells of hometown and spring

不善饮者

一家临街小酒馆
我独饮，秋风一杯夜雨一杯
窗外，哒哒马蹄声
由远及近，又及远

掌柜说
义军的骑兵团正开赴前线

真烦躁啊这无休止被
同一粒绳结所线性的世界
我将仆倒于哪一杯中

如果换到街对面
另一家酒馆
马蹄声是否会掉个方向
由近及远，又及近

掌柜是否会说
叛军正凯旋归来

真烦躁啊明天我就把
你让我保守的秘密说给X
再让Y把它倒给你

Not a Good Drinker

In a small curbside restaurant
I drank alone, one cup of autumn wind after another of night rain
Outside the window, the hooves of a horse
From far to near, then far again

The restaurateur said
The calvary regiment of the rebels were marching to the front

I'm so bothered with this world
Endlessly linearized by the grain of a knot
That I wonder which cup I'll fall into

What if I swap restaurants
By going to the other one across the street
Would the hooves of the horse change directions
Going from near to far, and near again

And the restaurateur would say
The rebels were coming back, with flying colours

Oh, I'm so bothered that tomorrow I'll
Tell X of the secret you want me to keep
And get Y to pour it into you

春天的非赞美诗

我在春天的夜晚穿行
也许刚下过一场雨
土地里拱起一阵泥土的腥味
情欲在体内发出吱吱的叫声
街角遇几老友，彼此打量宛如新交
一老鳏夫朝着粉巷儿疾走
噢，春天，所有感官都被叫醒
我的言说却愈发含混
前几天我夜登望牛墩，希望在高处
在你们和他们的
时间之外，一窥它的真面目
却看到东边的贲门，西边的盲肠
南边的脾，北边的肝脏
原来宇宙只是春天的一只胃
那一刻我惊呆了
下山后给远方的友人写信——
我看到星空端坐在春天的腹腔中
我只是它众多杯盏中的一只
为它盛满情欲，爱恨，死亡体验
原以为有一些属于我自己
原以为了解它的一些秘密……

A Non-hymn in Spring

I was walking through the spring night
Maybe it had just rained
When a smell of soil erupted from the earth
And desire was squeaking inside the body
I met a few old friends around the street corner, sizing each other up, like new
    friends
An old widower was walking in hurried steps into a powder lane
Oh, spring, all the senses were woken up
While my speech became even more muddled
A few days ago, when I went to Cow-Watching Mound, I hoped that on high
Beyond your time
And theirs, I could glimpse its true features
But all I could see was the cardia in the east, the cecum in the west
The spleen in the south and the liver in the north
And I realized that the universe was the stomach of the spring
It was in that instant that I was amazed
After I came down the mound, I wrote a letter to a friend far away—
I saw the firmament seated in the abdomen of the spring
I am but one cup of its many cups and glasses
Filling it with desire, love/hate, and an experience of death
Despite the fact that I had thought some of it belonged to myself
And that I knew a number of its secrets...

写于慕尼黑一家中餐馆的三楼露台

电车拐弯处即是
冬天的中心
再向前三百米
它将遇到一片教堂的阴影
在那里它必须变换
一种速度
才能克服长时间单一节奏
所积聚的

厌倦，还来自星期日上午
空无一人的慕尼黑大街
厚厚的遮光帘后面
羁旅者为了更好地梦见祖国
不惜删除了所有的电话号码
哦，我也曾有大雪纷飞的

祖国，究竟是一个名词还是形容词
再过三天，我也要回到
一个叫做祖国的地方
但即使离开得再久一些，那里也没有我
迫切想亲近的人或事物
我只有在心里将它默读数遍
直到读出它深深的荒谬
哦，所谓乡愁，从来都只是一滩

狗屎，莫过于我
只爱着自己不喜欢的
即使回到人声鼎沸的母语中
我有多热爱她们的模样
就有多厌恶她们的灵魂，但灵魂
在故国失去在异乡又如何召回

Written in the balcony on the third floor of a Chinese restaurant in Munich

It's the centre of the winter
Where the tram turns the corner
Three hundred metres further onwards
It'll meet with the shadow of a church
There it must change
Into another speed
To overcome the boredom
Accumulated by the monotonous rhythm over a long

Time, which also comes from the deserted street
Of Munich on a Sunday morning
Behind the heavy blinds
The sojourner, to better dream of his motherland
Deletes all the phone numbers
Oh, I also had a motherland in flying

Snow, was it a noun or an adjective
In three days, I'll also return
To a place called Motherland
But even if I stay longer away there are no people or things
I urgently want to get close to
All I do is keep reading it in silence in my heart for a few times
Until I read deep absurdity into it
Aw, the so-called nostalgia is but a pool of

Dogshit, not as good as my
Love of whatever I don't like
Even if I return to the noisy mother tongue
The more I like their ways
The more I detest their souls but if a soul
Is lost in one's native country how can you recall it in an alien land

电车过处，一群鸽子
缓缓飞过阿萨尔河上的桥梁
在它漫不经心的起落之间
在阿萨尔河闪闪的波光里
我终于认出了我的孤独
它不属于过去也不属于未来
令我再度，硬起了心肠

Where the tram went past, a group of doves
Slowly flew over the bridge on the Isar
In their careless flight up and down
And in the light of the ripples in the Isar
I ended up recognizing my solitude
It, not belonging to the past nor to the future
Made me steel my heart, once again

在福州

喜来登酒店在哪里？
就在国际会展中心边上
国际会展中心在哪里？
就在喜来登酒店旁边

从市中心出发
几十公里的荒郊野岭
暴露了城市的规划和野心
"最多再二十年吧"
中年司机话语低沉

开阔的大堂和走廊
几百平米的房间
我从沙发辗转到床，再从床
散步到浴室，最后打盹于阳台一把躺椅
群山之脊在雾霭中消隐
不再敢盲目地诅咒，也不敢再轻佻地赞美

偌大酒店似乎只我一名住客
被自由所囚者，足以操死
一头牛，一个皮肤粗糙的男人
我承认有一刻我出现了幻听
地底岩浆奔涌
隔壁情侣呢喃
但老福州，我还从未读过你充满灵异的城史

像一个与世无争的人，一个
大隐隐于镜的人
在女儿出生前三个月
我掐断所有网络
放弃全部旅行计划
我需要渐渐爱上这个国家

In Fuzhou

Where is Sheraton Hotel?
Right on the edge of International Exhibition Centre
Where is International Exhibition Centre?
Just next to Sheraton Hotel

When you departed from the centre of the city
Kilometres of wilderness
Revealed the city's planning and ambition
'At most, another twenty years'
The middle-age driver spoke in a low voice

The vast hall and the corridors
A room of hundred square metres
I moved from the sofa to the bed, and from the bed
To the bathroom, until I sat dozing in a recliner in the balcony
As the ridges of the mountains were disappearing in the smog
I no longer dare curse blindly nor dare I praise frivolously

The huge hotel seemed to have me alone, the single guest
Those imprisoned by freedom had got enough to fuck a cow
Dead, a man with rough skin
I admit that, for a moment, I heard voices
Magma surging from the bottom of the earth
Lovers whispering next door
But, Old Fuzhou, I have never read the history of you filled with the supernatural

Like someone holding aloof from the rest of the world, a hermit
That takes refuge in a mirror
I, three months before my daughter was born
Cut off all the network
And gave up all my planned travels
As I need to gradually fall in love with this country

蚊子是唯一的玩物
阳台上，竹林边
我已双手拍死8只，越发精于
预判它们的飞行线路，一飞即毙
就像出租车司机预判城市的命运

喜来登酒店在哪里？
就在国际会展中心边上
国际会展中心在哪里？
就在喜来登酒店旁边

Mosquitoes are the only playthings
In the balcony and at the edge of the bamboo
I had squashed 8 to death, getting better at
Pre-judging their routes of flight, killing them as they took flight
Like the driver who pre-judged the fate of the city

Where is Sheraton Hotel?
Right on the edge of International Exhibition Centre
Where is International Exhibition Centre?
Just next to Sheraton Hotel

午夜梦醒，依旧无法驾驭这混乱的生活

第一次操爱都没激动的女人
此刻躺在一块画布上
（也可能是一面山坡）

她该有何等黯淡的童年
才让杜鹃收起喉咙
山脚下的火车都不愿为她提速

端午节刚过，我的前妻
就在QQ上签名
"一场雨后，秋天似乎来了"

啊如果秋风乍起
一点点吹掉我们
一起生活过十年的痕迹

必须去一趟郊外，必须
给秘书发邮件
让她明天穿那件印花短裙

诗人们越写越臭
我只有重新拿起笔
继续在黑暗中教他们写作

直到父亲来电，他说老家最后一户人家
也于昨夜搬离
啊满满一背囊故乡的明月和骨灰

Waking up from a midnight dream, still unable to control this confused life

The woman that wasn't even excited with the first fuck
Is now lying on a canvas
(could also be a slope)

What dark childhood she must have had
To cause the cuckoo to fold its throat
And the train at the foot of the hill to stop speeding up for her

Shortly after the Dragon Boat Festival, my ex-wife
Signed on QQ, with this
'The autumn seems to have arrived, after the rain'

If only the autumn wind, rising
Could blow away the traces
Of our lives lived together for ten years

Must go outside the city, must
Email my secretary
And get her to wear that printed short skirt tomorrow

The more they write, the more the poets stink
All I have to do is pick up my pen again
And, in the dark, teach them how to write

Till father called, saying that the last household at his old home
Had moved last night
Ah, a full sack of native home's moon and bone ashes

老婆说题目就叫平安夜吧

一只幼虫
被我用烟头
在半平方的水泥台面上
围追堵截

通红的烟头
等候在它逃亡的前方
逼它一次次折返

施虐和末日的
气息，交织

从厕所出来
我就在盥洗室的台面上
看到它了

耗尽最后的
八支香烟
我小心翼翼
不把烟灰抖落到它身上

女儿出生后
我就再也没有踩死过
一只蚂蚁

从善和幸存的
喜悦，弥漫

唱诗班的歌声在远处响起
主的光辉已经降临在钟塔上
平安夜，写字楼早已空空

My wife said: Just call it 'Silent Night'

A larva
Was being chased
By me with a cigarette-butt
On the half-square-metre benchtop

The butt, burning red
Was waiting in the front where it was running to
For it to return again and again

The aroma of sadism and
Doomsday, intertwined

After I came out of the loo
I saw it on the benchtop
Of the toilet

After I exhausted the last
Eight cigarettes
I, carefully
Avoided shaking the ashes over it

After my daughter was born
I have never trodden
On a single ant

Joy of turning over a new leaf
And survival, diffusing

The choir began singing in the distance
As Lord's light descended over the clock tower
On silent night, the office building was long deserted

新闻联播的片头曲
比往日嘹亮
头条就是
一场大浩劫与两名幸存者

The opening theme of Xinwen Lianbo (News Simulcast)
Was louder than before
The headlines being
The only two survivors of a catastrophe

人物（376）

百岁老头。长寿
源于他身体里七十多种癌症
娘胎里就得了三种。此后
每隔两年新增一种
除了绝症他没得过其它病
人越活越年轻
胃口越来越好，甚至能
大坨大坨屙出夜色
他走过的土地长不出庄家
他吐纳过的空气有人提炼出毒品
今年又添两种
头发癌，手指癌
只要中指朝上
头发就会跟着竖起来
天空就会骤降硫酸雨
因此今年的庆祝他想搞得再隆重点
地点也从食堂搬到广场

A Character (376)

A man a century old. Longevity
Originates from more than seventy cancers in his body
Three of which acquired inside his mother's belly, and, subsequently
He has a new one every two years
Except anything terminal
The longer he lives the younger he becomes
And the better appetite, to the degree that he is able
To produce chunks of night colours
Wherever he passes no crop grows
And people can refine drugs out of his breaths
Two more cancers he has produced this year
Hair cancer and finger cancer
Once he gives you the finger
His hair stands with it
And a sudden acid rain will fall
For this reason, he thinks of mounting a grander celebration this year
Moving from the canteen to the square

在延安

凌晨的酒店前台
一个背影姣好的女子
酷似我客居之地那些
湖南或湖北籍骚货
噢，国庆假期，革命老区
此刻瓜果飘香，秋高气爽
作为旅行目的地
颇符合黄金周的逻辑，季节
深藏不露的胃口
她不停与服务员交涉
抑制不住独自远行的激动
（也许在讨价还价又也许是
咨询明天的游玩路线）

无知的骚娘们又开始朝延安扎堆
相似的历史总有隐秘的相通之处
我在大堂暗处盯着她
像一个生活的老手，或
失意者
再也不能被他人的快乐
所感染
我看见她阔腿裤里的屁股蛋子
在昏暗的灯光下微微晃动
如果换成超短裙或紧身裤
定会更性感一些
但即使她天亮之后就奔赴梁家河
也无法治愈我的绝症
——对人类不举，当然对牲口
也不举

In Yan'an

In the wee hours, at the hotel front desk
A girl whose back looked good
Very much resembled those pussy skanks from Hubei or Hunan
In the places where I sojourned
Oh, during National Day holiday and in the old revolutionary base area
At this time of year, fruit smells good, the autumn is high and the air, crisp
As a tourist destination
It quite fits the logic of Golden Week, with the season's
Appetite, too deep for show
She kept arguing with the waitress
And couldn't contain her excitement over her journey alone
(she's probably bargaining or possibly
Checking about her sightseeing tours tomorrow)

The ignorant pussy skanks have now begun crowding upon Yan'an
Similar histories always with secretive places of access
Watching her from a dark corner in the hall
I looked like an old hand at life or
A loser
No longer capable of being affected
By other people's pleasure
I could see the bums inside her voluminous trousers
Slightly shaking in the dim light
If she changed into a shorter skirt or tighter-fitting trousers
It would be sexier
But even if she rushed to Liangjiahe after daybreak
It would not cure me of my terminal illness
—my inability to get erected at hu(wo)manity and, of course
To animals, too

Three Australian Poems: A Sequence

小便后抖鸡巴的动作看上去像一个隐喻

一条黝黑的鸡巴
在一泡尿后抖了十几下

不好意思看他的脸
因此我不敢断定就是位黑人兄弟

如果白人长了条黑鸡巴
那就变成另一个隐喻

但我只抖了三下，心情差的时候
我往往只抖一两下，甚至，不洗手

小便后不抖鸡巴的人，一定是
内向之人，爱得轻浮之人

悬挂在洗手台上方的风景
看上去像无辜的亚拉河
（莫名其妙令我悲伤）

而它依然在抖，麻木被空气传导
迫使我再度看清自己的厌倦、虚无，以及

失语症。如果有一天我突然恢复了言说
一定是兄弟们发明了一种新的季节

隆重地
向我发来请柬

The way he shook his dick after pissing looked like a metaphor

A black dick
Shook more than a dozen times after pissing

I was too embarrassed to look at his face
And, for that reason, I dared not assume that it was that of a black brother's

If a white man has a black dick
It'll become another metaphor

But I only shook mine three times and when I am not in the mood
I normally shake it twice, not even washing my hands

One who doesn't shake his dick after pissing must be
An introvert, a frivolous guy with love

The landscape hanging over the washbasin
Looks like the innocent Yarra River
(and saddened me for no reason at all)

But it kept shaking, a sense of numbness conveyed by the air
Forcing me to once again see my own weariness, nihility and

Aphasia. If one day I suddenly recoup my speech abilities
It must be because my brothers have invented a new season

Solemnly
Sending me an invite

蓝山国家公园

老灿
悉尼我就不来了
因此不能陪你们去蓝山公园
蓝山，真是一个好听的名字
你们多拍些照片
忘掉那些烦心事
把嫂子和孩子们都装进镜头
当新一年的春天覆盖北半球
朋友们都围着手机
夸南太平洋辽阔
夸嫂子漂亮，孩子可爱
由衷地笑出声来

Blue Mountains National Park

Old Can
I'm not going to Sydney now
So can't go to Blue Mountains National Park with you
Blue Mountains, what a good-sounding name
You take lots of photographs
Forget the stuff that bothers you
And put your wife and kids in the lens
When the spring of a new year covers up the northern hemisphere
That's when friends surround the mobile phone
Praising how vast the Southern Pacific is
How pretty your wife is and how lovely your kids are
Bursting into laughter from the bottom of their hearts

亚拉河

一干东亚模样的人来到亚拉河边
朝着河面指指点点

"原来澳洲的河也这么黑啊
连海鸥都照不见自己的影子"

本地人则坐在堤岸靠里一些的咖啡厅的阴凉里
没人朝河的方向瞟上一眼

"亚拉河是一条脏分分的黑河"
风一样在地球上流转

吸引更多的东亚人来到河边
对着河面指指点点

"原来亚拉河比XX河也好不了多少呀
连乌鸦都照不见它的影子"

然后他们心满意足地走进咖啡厅
在那些阳光直射的桌子上坐了下来

The Yarra River

A gang of East-Asian-looking people arrived at the side of the Yarra River
Pointing at it

'It so happens that even the Australian river is so dark
That seagulls can't see their own reflections'

While the locals sat in the shade of the café further away from the bank
No one glancing in the direction of the river

'The Yarra is a dirty, black river'
Flowing on the globe, like wind

Attracting more East Asians to the riverbank
Pointing at the river

'It so happens that the Yarra is no better than the so and so river
No even the magpies can see their shadows in it'

Satisfied, they went into the café
And sat down at the tables where the sun struck down straight

祭奠：写给姐姐和哥哥的一首诗

恍如从来没有存在
甚至未曾拥有一个正式名字
也没有留下任何影像
就连父母，也很多年不再提起
但我确实有过
一个姐姐，和一个哥哥
为什么我在不爱人类之后
才想起爱你们
在有了女儿和儿子之后
才尝试想象你们的模样
我的哥哥，生于1967死于1967
母亲说，也许是肺炎，老咳嗽
我的姐姐，生于1968腊月
1969腊月死于
一个乡村赤脚医生的青霉素过敏
母亲说，你学话早
死前一个月
就对着窗台的花猫喊喵喵
母亲曾向我说起
你咽气前小腿挣扎的样子
你们都生于一个叫白季茆的村庄
死后也葬于此地
噢，所谓葬，就是将小小的尸体
胡乱扔上山岗
一辈子只出现在一个村庄
一辈子只见过四位家人
噢，应该再加上那位赤脚医生
是否也是一种纯粹的人生
哥哥，和姐姐
我在你们死后出生
至今已活了四十多年

A memorial ceremony, with a poem for my older sister and brother

It's almost as if they had never existed
Never even owned an official name
Never had any photographs of themselves left
Not even our parents mentioned them for many years
But I did have
An older sister, and brother
Why did I remember to love you
When I stopped loving human beings
Why did I try to remember your features
After I had my daughter and my son
My older brother, born in 1967 and died in 1967
According to mother, of pneumonia, coughing constantly
My older sister, born in the twelfth lunar month of 1968
And died in the twelfth lunar month of 1969
Of penicillin allergy administered by a village barefoot doctor
Mother said: You learned to speak early
As you mewed at the flowery cat on the windowsill
A month before death
Mother told me
How your little legs were struggling before you breathed your last
Both of you died in a village called Baijimao
And were *zang*ed there after death
Oh, when we talk about 'zang', it's randomly throwing
The little bodies on the hill's ridge
That happened only in a village in one lifetime
One saw only four family members in one lifetime
Oh, one should throw in the barefoot doctor
Can't that count as a pure life
Older brother, and sister
I was born after you died
And have lived for over forty years

我替你们，在这世界
行走，观看，感受它的冷暖
我想象过爱你们的感觉
应该就像爱我们的父亲和母亲
爱我的女儿和儿子
（也就是你们的侄子和侄女）
但我永远想像不出
被一个哥哥和姐姐
宠爱或管教
噢，亲爱的哥哥和姐姐
请原谅我在不爱这世界之后才尝试爱你们
在有了儿子和女儿之后
才想到为你们写一首诗
并试图让你们
在这首诗里短暂复活
像一截纸做的墓碑
简短，无力
在风中飞舞
旋即飘向那无边的黑暗

I, on behalf of you, in this world
Walk and watch, feeling its cold and warmth
I did imagine the feeling of love for you
That should resemble my love for our father and mother
And for my daughter and son
(your nephew and niece)
Although I can never imagine
How it feels to be pampered or disciplined
By an older brother and sister
Oh, my dear older brother and sister
Please forgive me for trying to love you after I stopped loving this world
And for thinking of writing a poem for you
After I had my son and daughter
And trying to revive you
Temporarily in this poem
Like a gravestone made of paper
Short, powerless
Dancing in the wind
Before drifting towards the endless darkness

白季峁，不仅仅是一部饥饿史

——为白季峁写首诗，愿父母健康长寿，家乡父老平安

1.
我出生于陕西省延安地区
子长县涧峪岔公社
杨渠大队白季峁生产队

八十年代初
涧峪岔公社被拆分为两个乡
我就成了陕西省延安地区子长县
高台乡杨渠大队白季峁自然村

九十年代
延安行署又变成延安市

确切的来历
稳固的籍贯
映衬我幽暗的成长史
越来越含混的心灵

2.
白季峁全村十几户人家
大部分姓蔡
鼎盛时村民五六十口

左侧山梁上
巉岩突起处是一座
破败的龙王庙

沟底一眼水井
日产十几担水

Baijimao, Not Just a History of Famine

—A poem for Baijimao to wish health and longevity to my parents and peace to
my home village people

1.
I was born in Baijimao Production Team, Yangqu Brigade
Jianyucha Commune, Zichang county
Yan'an prefecture, Shaanxi province

In the early 1980s
Jianyucha Commune was divided into two towns
When I became the natural village of Baijimao, Yangqu Brigade, Gaotai Town
Zichang county, Yan'an prefecture, Shaanxi province

In the 1990s
Yan'an Administrative Office became Yan'an city

An accurate origin
And a stable place of origin
Are reflected in the increasingly confused heart
Of my dark history of growth

2.
Most of the dozen households in the village of Baijimao
Are surnamed Cai
At its height, there was a population of 50 to 60 villagers

On the jutting rock
On the left ridge of the mountain
There was a ramshackle Dragon King Temple

There was a well at the bottom of the valley
That generated more than two dozen buckets of water per day

饮着全村老少
和牲口

我多次看见
羊群在井里撒尿

3.
没有族谱
和祖坟

一些新坟和次新坟
随意散落在脑畔山上

北风呼呼吹着招魂幡，和
丧棍上的纸屑

用不了多久它们
就会被风沙抹平

我不知道太爷爷的名字
更没有见过他的坟包

白季峁渺小到
不需要任何传承

4.
母亲每天披星上山
荷月归来

半傻的生产队长
喊着号子

生我前一天还在人民公社的山上
不到满月又回到人民公社的田里

That fed the whole village
And its cattle

On many occasions, I saw
The sheep piss into the well

3.
There was no family history record book
And no ancestral grave

A number of new graves and secondary new graves
Are scattered on the Naopanshan Mountain at random

A northerly noisily blows the homing banners, and
The shreds of paper around the sticks of bereavement

It won't be long
Before they are wiped flat by the wind and sands

I do not know the name of my great grandfather
Nor have I seen his grave

Baijimao is so tiny
It needs no inheritance

4.
Mother went up the hill daily, stars on her back
And came back, moon on her hoe

As the half-silly production team leader
Was shouting a work song

A day before she gave me birth she was still on the mountain of People's Commune
And before the month ran out she returned to the field of the same

母亲全年无休但全年
吃不上一顿饱饭

这个事实
比荒诞本身还要荒谬

5.
天一黑就嚎

五岁以前，每个夜晚
我都在嚎哭中度过

饥饿的感觉
不疼痛
亦不悲伤

一截肠子
挂在风中
被鞭子抽打

母亲站在灶台
跺着脚诅咒
我的爷爷啊求你别哭了
睡着就不饿了

我讨厌母亲的腔调
但我佩服生活赐予她的经验
确实，只要睡着
醒来后就真没那么饿了

6.
我在窑洞的土炕上嚎
狐狸在远山嚎
奇怪子在门前大槐树上嚎

Mother had no rest for the whole year but for the whole year
She never ate her fill

This fact
Is more absurd than absurdities

5.
I howled as soon as darkness fell

Before I turned five, I spent every
Night howling

The sense of hunger
Was not painful
Or sad

A section of the intestine
Hanging in the wind
Was whipped by the wind

Mother stood at the stove
Stamping her feet and cursing
My granddad, I beg you to stop crying
You won't feel hungry when you fall asleep

I hate Mother's tone
But I admire her for her experience given by life
Once you fell asleep, you wouldn't
Feel hungry after you woke up, that's true

6.
I howled on the earthen kang in the cave dwelling
And the foxes were howling in the distant mountain
Strange Kid was howling in the big locust tree in front of our house

母亲在灶台前
跺着脚诅咒

煤油灯昏黄闪烁
将母亲瘦俏的影子
投到泥巴墙上

白季峁把猫头鹰
叫做奇怪子
一种不祥鸟

7.
被饥饿摧残过的身体
依然坚挺
被饥饿蹂躏过的心灵
似乎也没留下什么阴影

只是女儿出生后
我经常被代入一种
身份置换后的场景

假如我是我母亲
女儿是我

女儿整夜嚎哭，喊饿
而我翻箱倒柜也找不到
一粒米，一颗野菜

母亲也饿啊
但我相信这悲伤
足以将她喂个半饱

8.
十二岁第一次吃肉

And Mother stood before the stove
Stamping her feet and cursing

The kerosene light, dim and flickering
Cast the thin and pretty shadow of Mother
Onto the mud wall

In Baijimao, an owl
Is called 'Strange Kid'
An unlucky bird

7.
My body, ravaged by hunger
Remains strong
And my heart, downtrodden by hunger
Does not seem to have any shadows, either

Except that after my daughter was born
I constantly feel as if I was placed in a situation
Of replaced identity

I being my mother
She, me

Every night she howled, crying she's hungry
I ransacked everything without being able to find
A grain of rice or a stem of wild vegetables

Mother was also hungry
But I believe that the hunger
Was enough to feed her half full

8.
At twelve, I ate pork for the first time

十五岁前没见过大米
十八岁前没见过鱼

野菜只有两种
苦菜早被拔光
槐花花期太短

我站在村头
大口饮风
看到白季岽瘦如纸片
上下翻飞

9.
山丹丹和打碗碗花
开满高原的春天

即使最饥荒的年份
它们也在每一片土地上
怒放

可惜都不能果腹

10.
二毛子死了
死于小河沟边上
睡着时被狼叼走
只留下一只小鞋
二老拐死了
死于到山背后拾柴
跌进一米深的天窖
那是暴雨冲积成的土坑
在黄土高原司空见惯
二叔死了
死于生产队收工路上

Before fifteen, I had not seen rice
Before eighteen, I had not seen fish

There are two kinds of wild vegetables
Kucai, bitter vegetables, had long been uprooted
While huaihua, black locust flowers, had too short a flowering period

I stood at the end of the village
Drinking mouthfuls of wind
And saw Baijimao, thin as a piece of paper
Fluttering up and down

9.
The spring fills the plateau
With Morningstar lilies and beat-bowl-bowl flowers

There's a fury of them
On every inch of the land
Even in the hungriest year

The only pity is that you can't eat them

10.
Second Hair died
On the edge of the river ditch
Taken by the wolves when asleep
Leaving only a small shoe behind
Second Old Stick died
While collecting firewood on the back of the mountain
As he fell into a sky-cave one meter deep
A pit formed by rainstorms
A common sight on the plateau
Second Uncle died
On his way home when the production team finished work

掉队后滑下两米高的土坡
翌日清晨发现他雪地上的尸体
朝着村庄方向
蠕动了二三十米

白季岽从来骄傲宣称
毛时代也没有饿死一个人

11.
漫长的饥饿的童年
却有一次差点被撑死的记录

母亲说那天我吃了
三十几个鸡蛋泡泡
一种鸡蛋和面粉的油炸食品
进入胃后会急速膨胀

午夜，熟睡中的我
突然站起
再躺下
再站起
如是重复几十遍

母亲和奶奶被吓得半死
安静地坐我身边
等着我死去
或者
侥幸活下来
而我浑然不知

白季岽的词典里
从没有医院或医药这个词

As he fell behind and down the slope two metres high
When they found his body on the snow early next morning
It had moved twenty to thirty metres
In the direction of the village

Baijimao, though, is always proud enough to proclaim
That no one died of starvation under Mao

11.
In the long and hungry childhood
There was a record of me dying nearly of overeating

According to Mother, I had eaten that day
More than 30 egg bubbles
A stir-fried foodstuff, mixed with eggs and flour
That would rapidly expand in the stomach

In the middle of the night, I rose from a sound sleep
On a sudden
Before I lay down
And stood up again
Repeatedly, for scores of times

Scaring Mother and Grandmother to death
Waiting by my side
For me to die
Or to survive by accident
While I had no idea what was going on

In the dictionary of Baijimao
There are no such words as hospital or medications

12.
陕北白季峁村
全年人均口粮4公斤
八成以上粗粮
浮肿率百分之百

1977年的陕北
相对风调雨顺的一年

以上信息
见于1977
新华社内参

13.
4公斤除以365天
等于10.95克
等于几十只
倒扣的空碗
几十只
悬吊起来的胃
装不下一粒羊粪
一声
鸟的悲鸣

14.
在我从饥饿童年
走向富翁中年的过程里
白季峁已成荒村
废弃的窑洞和水井
祖先的尸骨
都即将被流沙彻底掩埋

我诅咒贫困但拒绝歌颂
富裕

12.
In the village of Baijimao, in northern Shaanxi
The per capita ration per annum was 4 kilograms
80% of that coarse grains
With a 100% of edema rate

Northern Shaanxi in 1977
Was relatively rain-smooth

Please refer to
The internal Reference of Xinhua News Agency, 1977
For the information above

13.
4 kilograms divided by 365 days
Is 10.95 grams
Equivalent to scores of bowls
Turned upside down
Scores of suspended stomachs
That can't even hold a single pellet of sheep's shit
And a single sound
Of the bird's sad song

14.
In the process in which I moved from a hungry childhood
To a rich middle age
Baijimao has become deserted
With abandoned cave dwellings and wells
The bones of the ancestors
Soon to be thoroughly buried by the quicksand

While I curse poverty I refuse to sing of
Riches

潜意识里我对任何
优越生活，含有敌意

我甚至讨厌富这个汉字
生来斜乜的眼神
豁嘴藏不住两颗大金牙

真是对不起啊

但我对不起谁
我为何要说对不起

也许只有白季朏知道
更也许白季朏也不知道

Subconsciously, I am
Hostile towards any well-off life

I even hate the word 'rich'
Born cross-eyed
And harelipped, with two big unconcealable gold teeth

I really am sorry

But sorry to whom
And why did I say 'sorry'

Perhaps only Baijimao knows
Perhaps not even Baijimao knows

10月4日下午

东海商场门口的星巴克
顾客寥寥
带有明显的节日印记
我在临街一张桌上
坐下来，点燃一支烟
正在犹豫要不要来杯咖啡
（事实上我只是想抽支烟）
女儿突然从商场里冲出来
一边喊爸爸一边抱紧我的左腿
抵消了我一部分的不好意思
紧接着，儿子也从商场跑了出来
抱紧我的右腿
抵消了我另一部分的不好意思
带孩子的男人，此时可以
心安理得的只坐他们的椅子
不消费他们的咖啡
我注意到阳光很好
气温不冷不热
随手翻翻朋友圈
诗人们又在争吵
才气矮于野心
只能一次次暴露他们的
土鳖和无知
口语是一杆虚枪
民间也只是在野党
我只关心这天气
这难得的稀疏的车流
行人三三两两，脚步不疾不徐
国庆假期的第四天
我感到最爽的一天

One Afternoon on October 4th

At the Starbucks near the entrance of East Ocean Shopping Mall
There were few customers
There were obvious signs of a festival
I sat down at a table
On the kerbside and lit a cigarette
Just as I was wondering if I should have a coffee
(while in fact I was only meaning to smoke a ciggy)
My daughter rushed out of the mall
Crying 'Dad' as she held my left leg in a tight hug
And that eased part of my embarrassment
Shortly after, my son also rushed out of the mall
And tightly held my right leg
And that eased another part of my embarrassment
A man with kids could now
Sit in their chair at ease
Without having to order their coffee
Right then I noticed that the sunlight was good
And the temperature was neither cold nor hot
Randomly, I had a look at the WeChat Moments
And could see that poets were fighting again
Their talent shorter than their ambitions
Exposing, again and again, their own
Earth-turtle status and ignorance
Mouth language is but a fake gun
And *minjian* is but an opposition party
All I care about is the weather
Under which the traffic is sparse, quite rare
Pedestrians in twos and threes, their footsteps sluggish
The fourth day of National Day holiday
Is the coolest one, I feel

母亲说一个冬天没下一粒雪地都快干死了

我想带女儿
回陕北老家
看雪
父亲
也就是女儿的爷爷
天天站在院子里
猫头鹰一样
张望着天空
终于他喊
下雪了，快来看
女儿在雪地里
雀跃，任雪花
落在她的
帽子上，嘴巴里
后来
女儿要求和爷爷打雪仗
被拒绝
女儿说，如果不打雪仗
这雪等于没下
至少下得不完整
但我不忍心告诉她
对于一个生长在北方的人
从来不打雪仗
他们被雪霁后的泥泞
脏怕了

According to Mother, there has not been a single flake of snow all winter and the field is nearly dried to death

I'm going to take my daughter
Back to my old home in northern Shaanxi
To see the snow
Father
My daughter's granddad
Stands daily in the courtyard
Watching the sky
Like an owl
Until he cries:
It's snowing. Come. Quick
My daughter is frolicking
On the snow, letting the snowflakes
Fall on her
Hat and into her mouth
Then she wants to fight a snow war with granddad
But is refused
My daughter says: If you don't fight a snow war
It's as if the snow had never snowed
Or at least not completely
But I didn't have the heart to tell her
For someone born in the north
They never fight a snow war
As they are scared of
The mud after the snow stops

春天，NO YUAN 了

来自利雅得的两架
私人飞机，于凌晨时分
先后降落伊斯坦布尔
一刻钟之前
塔台和跑道的灯光，被关闭
夜色恩爱、慈祥，包裹着
杀心和骨锯，开始盲降
（哦人类请允许我
闭上眼睛抓紧扶手）

包括保镖，特种兵，情报人员，法医
在内，一行15人，搭乘外交牌照汽车
疾疾驶入沙特驻伊领事馆
移居美国的沙特阿拉伯记者
异见人士，专栏作家，杠精，轴人
然后就消失了
让等在领馆门外的未婚妻
一直站到第二天黎明
（哦人类请允许我感到腿麻）

使馆区的居民没听到惨叫
现场没留下一滴血
（哦人类如果你们再多付三倍酬劳
清洁工能将上帝也融入一滴药水）
也就在这一天
中国管股票的主席说，春天不远了
他说到春天，然后他说，不远了

Spring, and No Yuan

Two private planes from
Riyadh, in the small hours
Landed, one after the other, in Istanbul
But a quarter of an hour ago
The tower and the runway lights had been switched off
The colours of the night were loving and kind, wrapping up
The killing heart and the bone as the plane began landing blind
(Ah, mankind, please allow me
To hold onto the railing, my eyes closed)

A group of 15, including the bodyguards, special forces, intelligence officers
And forensic doctors, riding in a vehicle with a foreign diplomatic number plate
Rushed into the Saudi consulate in Istanbul
When the Saudi journalist, a migrant to America
Dissident, columnist, troll and axis man
Disappeared
His fiancée kept waiting outside the consulate
Till dawn
(Oh, mankind, please allow me to feel numb in my legs)

Residents in the embassy district didn't hear any shrieks
No blood was left on the site
(Oh, mankind, if you pay a triple payment on top of what's paid
Cleaners might melt God in a drop of medicine)
And it's the same day
The chairman in charge of shares in China said: Spring is not far away
He talked about the spring, then he said: Not far away

灰

湛蓝太刺眼
和煦太瘙痒
碧绿太油腻
我从冬日午后的被窝醒来
瞥见窗外一片迷蒙
天地的大灰暗
包裹我内心的小灰暗
舒适，安心，妥帖
我知道我的乏味
源自内心的灰暗
但我不知道这内心的色彩
何时，又因何，而枯竭
此刻我们坐在港口大厦顶层
目睹人间繁华的灯火
如此天然地，成为我灰暗的一部分
小句说，你不是很爱女儿和儿子吗
是的，这爱，狭隘、强烈
但只能使我的灰暗升温
并不能刷新它的斑斓
就像我早已习惯寄居在这灰暗里
愧于面对天空，微风，草地
离开前她说明媚
噢，对，明媚
这正是我苦苦寻觅的一个词
只有它才能将这首诗点亮
那些湛蓝，和煦，苍翠欲滴
但小句啊你可记得
在我们交谈的两小时里
每遇词穷，头顶就有一架飞机飞过

Grey

Blue, too glaring
Genial, too itchy
Green, too oily
When I woke up from inside my quilt in the winter arvo
I glanced at the greyness outside the window
The greater grey of the sky and the earth
Wrapping up the smaller grey inside my heart
Comforting, peaceful, appropriate
I knew that my boredom
Came from my interior grey
But I did not know when the colour of my inner
Heart dried up, and why
Right now, I was sitting on the top floor of the harbour building
Watching the brilliantly illuminated world
So naturally turning into part of my greyness
Xiao Ju said: Don't you love your son and daughter?
Right. But this love, narrow, strong
Could only increase the temperature of my greyness
Without being able to update its splendour
It's as if I had long got used to residing in this greyness
Ashamed of facing the sky, the breeze, the lawn
Before her departure, she said: brightly
Oh, yes, brightly
That's the word I had been searching hard for
This word alone could brighten up the poem
Those words: blue, genial, dripping green
But, oh, Xiao Ju, do you remember
In the two hours in which we chatted
Whenever I ran out of words to say, there was an airplane flying overhead

五个问题也请朋友们作答

第一，已婚男人出轨是否有违道德
并请阐述您的理由
如果只是精神出轨呢
第二，假设有两个省长（副省长也行）
甲受贿一百万乙受贿一个亿
他俩谁被抓的风险高
如果都被抓了谁会被判得重
我曾问过几十个人
我的同事H总，选了一百万
某个内地的副市长选了一个亿
我的朋友而戈，在北京饭店，郑重的写下概率一样
第三，一个用方块字写诗的中国人移民去了新西兰
失去母语，忍受乡村生活广大的寂寞
如果换成你是否会像他这样选择
第四，未经孩子同意是否有权将他生出来
让他忍受疾病，压迫，以及令人窒息的死亡
（当然我不否认人生的快乐）
第五，如果你有一个七岁的女儿
第一堂课就背诵XXX语录
如果她还被班长勒索，漫长的校园霸凌
你会怎么办

Five Questions That I'd Like My Friends to Answer

First: If a married man has an affair, is that a breach of morality
And please explain your reasons
What if it is only a spiritual affair
Second: Assuming there are two provincial governors (deputy ones okay, too)
A is bribed with one million dollars and B, 100 million
Who runs a higher risk of being caught
Who receives a heavier sentence if caught
I asked scores of people
General Manager H, a colleague, said one million
A deputy mayor in inland China said 100 million
Er Ge, my friend, in Beijing Hotel, solemnly wrote: same probability
Third: A Chinese, writing poems in characters, went to New Zealand
Lost his mother tongue, and endured the vast solitude living in the country
If it were you, would you make the same choice as he did
Fourth: Without the child's agreement, do you have the right to give birth to him
To make him endure illnesses, oppression and suffocating death
(But of course I don't deny life's pleasures)
Fifth: If you had a daughter aged seven
Had to recite the remarks by XXX in her first classes
And if she had to be blackmailed, to suffer from long-term campus bullying
What would you do

他们连个像样的刑场都没有准备

雪，一节节
往墙根儿方向撤退
几天前，它曾貌似
完美地统治了世界
像一个伟大的罗马尼亚梦
覆盖着小便和呕吐物
可现在
土地正被阳光加速复辟
雪融之处
几片枯叶和鸡屎
露出来

带黑色毡帽的
独裁者
像一邻居老头儿
（甚至可用慈祥形容）
用左手
牵起他的老伴儿
（一点也不像帮凶）
几分钟前
这里曾搭起一个临时法庭
有过一场简易的死刑宣判
几位年轻士兵
跃跃欲试
用手套擦拭着枪管

炒豆子般的几声枪响
两只瘦小的身躯
朝左右两侧
缓缓倒了下去
血水和着泥泞

They had not even prepared a proper execution ground

Snow, section by section
Retreated towards the root of the wall
Days ago, it seemed to have
Perfectly ruled the world
Like a great Romanian dream
Covering up the piss and the vomit
But right now
The earth was speeding up its restoration with the sunshine
Where the snow was melting
Several withered leaves and chickenshit
Were exposed

The dictator
In a black felt hat
Like an old man next door
(could even be described as kindly)
Held his wife
With his left hand
(not at all like an accomplice)
Several minutes ago
A temporary execution ground had been set up here
With a simple announcement of death sentence
When several young soldiers
Were eager to give it a go
Wiping their gun barrels, with their gloves

Several shots, like the frying of beans
And two thin bodies
Fell towards the left and right
Slowly
Their blood mixed with mud

将罗马尼亚共和国最后的雪地
污染得不忍卒读
令我心头一颤的是
两只紧握的手
曾经的总统和第一夫人
就那么随意地
被地心引力分开了

一点也不诗意，不肃穆，不庄严
丝毫不像我想象中的枪决现场
他们连个像样的刑场都没有准备

Dirtying the last snow ground of the Republic of Romania
To an unreadable degree
What shivered my heart
Was the two hands held tightly together
The erstwhile president and the first lady
Separated so randomly
By the gravitational force

Not like poetry at all, not solemn, not dignified
Not at all like the imagined shooting scene
For they had not even prepared a proper execution ground

自白书

我的胸怀越来越狭窄
只容得下
风中一根麦芒
蓝天，白云，森林里的鸟鸣
我都容不下

我的爱越来越肤浅
曾经作为性的借口
现在只是性的佐料
而性就是操
但我操的力比多也正在衰减

我怀疑自己从未有过
你们歌颂的爱情
除了我的妻子
和偶尔牵挂的前妻
马路上那些淑女，骚货，假正经
我的性幻想越来越稍纵即逝

女儿和儿子之外我没有亲人
白季茆之外我没有故乡
我早已羞于承认
我是中国人，陕西人
更不用说傻逼陕北人

作为一个商人
我的生意伙伴只剩墙壁和大树
作为一个诗人
我早已懒得指导你们写作
但大树也在变坏
它诱我四季肥料

A Self-whitening Book

I am becoming increasingly narrower-minded
My mind can only contain
An awn of wheat in the wind
But it can't contain
The blue skies, white clouds and the birdsong in the forest

My love is increasingly becoming shallower
It used to be an excuse for sex
Now it's just an ingredient for it
And sex means fucking
But my libido for fucking is decreasing, too

I suspect I have never had
The kind of love you sing of
My sexual fantasies are increasingly transient
For the ladies, skanks and prudes on the streets
Except my wife
And my ex-wife, occasionally missed

I have no loved ones except my daughter and my son
I have no home except Baijimao
For long I have been ashamed of admitting
That I am Chinese, that I come from Shaanxi
And, least of all, that I am a fucking stupid northern Shaanxi'er

As a businessman
I have no business partners left except the walls and big trees
And as a poet
I have long been tired of telling you how to write
But the big trees are getting badder
As they induce me to give them four seasons of manure

报我三粒瘪果
酷似你们这些坏人类，这些
荒谬无知的美国人英国人俄罗斯人
瞧，外星人就要来收拾你们啦

For a return of three flattened pieces of fruit
Exactly like you the bad beings, the
Ignorant Americans, Brits, Russians
Look: Aliens are coming to fix you up now

纪念日，我不服气啊

一代人渐渐老了
在手机屏幕上再次看见他们
老的程度和我相仿
有几位看上去比我更加无望
我归结于被逃亡之后
常年在外的流离颠沛

三十年一晃就过了
时间真他妈快啊
快得像秋风停驻在高墙之外
像我们的爱情
永远来不及成熟

妻子这代不认识他们
甚至没听说过他们
妹妹这代瞪大眼睛
坚定认为这是个充满挑衅
和恶趣味的谎言

三代人分别被取消了
肉体，记忆和心灵
同一件机器，越来越精于伪装
在誓师队伍的背景里
它甚至打扮成一只宠物
依偎在少妇怀里吃奶
纸尿裤里拉出血和铁屑

我暗恋的小Z
喜欢乖巧的小奶狗
小N喜欢听话的小奶狗
小S则说我喜欢小狼狗

Memorial Day but I Won't Give Up, Not Yet

My generation is getting old
When I saw them again on my mobile phone
They looked about as old as me
A number of them more hopeless than me
Which I put down to their being exiled
Drifting from place to place abroad for years

Thirty years gone, in a flash
So fucking fast
As fast as the autumn wind stationed beyond the high wall
Like our love
That never matures in time

My wife's generation does not know them
Has not even heard of them
My younger sister's generation, wide-eyed
Is firmly of the opinion that that is a lie
Full of challenge and bad taste

The three generations respectively cancelled
Their bodies, their memories and their hearts
The same machine except that it is more skilled at camouflage
Against the background of the oath-taking team
It's even dressed as a pet
Sucking milk, nestled in the arms of a young woman
Shitting blood and iron filings in the paper diapers

Little Z that I was in secret love with
Loved clever little milk dogs
Little N loved little obedient milk dogs
Little S said she liked little wolfdogs

帅帅的，还有点凶

事实上狗狗们都是由
三十年前那一堆堆钢铁转世而来
它们恫吓过一代人
又被另一代人深深宠爱
舔食它们新鲜的精液
我将为我独知这个巨大的秘密
而震惊，担心被灭口

Ones that were smart, and a little aggressive

In fact, the dogs were
Reincarnated from the heaps of steel thirty years ago
They scared one generation
And they are deeply loved by another
Licking their fresh semen
I shall be shocked by this huge secret
That I alone know, and I worry that I might be destroyed

前妻家的门卡

钱包最里的夹层
发现一张前妻家的门卡
七年来我一次也没有用过
但莫名其妙已被磨损

离婚手续办妥后的2012年
前妻给我一张崭新的门卡
方便她不在时
我搬出私人物品

搬衣服仅用两周
搬书用了两年半
分割给我的小小轿车
承担了老鼠搬家的全部任务

书房里整面墙的书架
颅骨先抽出部分
胸腔里抽出部分
最后再断掉腿骨，和脚踝

貌似就要垮了
书架越来越寥落，冷清
偌大的书房只剩几十本书
我决定让它们留在原处

离开前在卧室，浴室，书房
分别巡视一圈
模拟我离开之后
她每日的生活和心境

A Door Card to My Ex-wife's Place

In the innermost fold of my wallet
I found a door card to my ex-wife's place
I had not used it for seven years
But it was, strangely, worn down

In 2012 when the divorce procedures were over
My ex gave me a brand-new door card
To make it convenient for me to move out
My own belongings in her absence

It took me two weeks to move my clothes
But it took two years and a half to move my books
The little car that was mine to have after the severance
Undertook all the tasks of a mouse removalist

To deal with the bookcase occupying the whole wall in the study
I first removed part of its skull
I then removed part of its chest
And, finally, I broke its legbones, and its ankles

Looking as if it was ready to collapse
The bookcase became hollower, colder
Only dozens of books were left in such a big study
And I decided to leave them where they were

Before I left, I went through the bedroom, the bathroom and the study
One by one, simulating the way she lived and felt on a daily basis
After I left

我们一起生活了十年的家
到处都留下我生活又搬走过的痕迹

钱包深处的门卡我至今未予归还
但愿我几乎搬空的书架现在已被重新填满

The home we had shared for ten years
Had traces everywhere, left of my living and moving

I still haven't returned the door card in the depths of my wallet
But I hope that the almost emptied bookcase has been refilled

在悬崖边写作

我的小小的书房
是阳台改的
而阳台
是开发商违章搭建的
（将一半算做赠送面积）
我曾亲眼目睹
国土局验收完毕后
他们连夜施工
将噪音死死捂进口罩
就这样我每天坐在
悬崖边写作
练习克服
对坠落的恐惧
像克制对人类的厌恶
像暗恋者克制表白
而坍塌总在下一秒到来
现在我邀请朋友们到我的书房
喝杯茶
再大声朗读这些
悬崖边的诗
我能想象
每读完一首
他们都会朝窗户下面
不安地张望

Writing on the Edge of the Cliff

My tiny little study
Was a transformation from the balcony
And the balcony
Was illegally constructed by the developer
(half of its area counted as for free)
I saw with my own eyes
How they started working overnight
Soon after it was checked and accepted by the Bureau of Land and Resources
Stuffing the noise hard underneath the masks
Thus I sat daily
Writing, on the edge of the cliff
Practising how to overcome
My fear of fall
Like how to overcome my disgust with the humanity
Like a secret lover, trying to overcome his confessions
And the collapse will always happen the next second
Now, I have invited my friends to come to my study
For a drink
And to read, in a loud voice
These poems on the edge of the cliff
I can imagine
That whenever they finish reading a poem
They'll nervously look down
Out the window

富人的悲伤

美女模特和她的
小奶狗老公
终于生出一个
赌王的长孙
我不仇富
模特中我甚至唯一喜欢她
我想说得是
小两口抱着襁褓中的婴儿
去探望爷爷
可爷爷没有回馈
预设中的欣喜
这个已经就木之人
每月花一亿港币续气
他不想撒手啊但思想
语言和情感都已经停止

美女模特
背过身去抹眼泪
的动作
突然击中了我
我相信他们探视爷爷
的行为
只是普通的人伦常情
不带有争财产的动机
但眼泪中有
也可能反过来成立

The Sadness of the Rich

The beautiful model and her
Ol' man, a little milk dog
Finally managed to give birth to the grandson
Of King of Gambling
I did not hate the rich
She was actually the only one of the models that I even liked
What I wanted to say was
When the two, holding the baby in their arms
Went to pay a visit to its granddad
He did not satisfy them
With the anticipated delight
The man, almost a mummy
Paid a monthly fee of 100 million Hong Kong dollars to keep breathing
He didn't want to go but his thoughts
His words and his feelings had all stopped

The way the model
Turned back to wipe
A tear
Suddenly hit me hard
As I believed that their visit to the granddad
Was normal human behaviour
Not motivated by a fight for property
Even though there might be that in her tears
As it would work in reverse

我热爱人类心灵中
温柔和悲伤的部分
如果他们没有
我宁愿杜撰一些
但富人的悲伤
有时比穷人
更令我动容

I love the tender and sad part
Of what is a human heart
I wish I could invent something
Even if they didn't think along those lines
But the sadness of the rich
Moves me more
Than that of the poor, sometimes

两棵树

我望着两棵树上
同样的烂果子
出神
这是两棵
科纲目门
完全不同的树
隐藏在地下的根系
和暴露在空气中的树冠
也完全不同
但枝头上挂着的果子
一样溃烂，流着
相同或相似的
脓水
这是人类最后一个秋天
地球上仅存两棵树
我在树下出神
我究竟该吃哪一棵呢
或者都不吃等着被
饿死

Two Trees

I watched the two trees
Fascinated
By their similar rotten fruit
These are two trees
Different in family, order, class and phylum
Their roots hidden underground
And their crowns, exposed in the air
Also completely different
But the fruit hanging on their branches
Was similarly rotten, running
With the same or similar
Pus
This is the final winter of mankind
The only two last surviving trees
I wondered under them
Which one I should eat first
Or if I should wait to die of starvation
Without eating either

南澳海边所见

一条黑色野狗
以强奸的手法
上了一条白色野狗
白狗半推半就
被抽插三下后
夹起尾巴跑开了
似我们熟悉的
某种场景（伎俩）
黑狗挺着鸡巴
起身狂追
将白狗摁在草丛
一顿狂操
我听到黑狗的满足
在胸腔里翻滚
白狗则一遍遍重复
不要停，不要停
这黑白交欢的过程
在南澳海边被我完整见证
和小区楼下常见的
宠物狗们，大有不同
相对于它们的
体面，尊雍，闲庭信步
熟练地克制性欲
我更被眼前这
原始，粗粝，热情狂野
所击中
它们牛逼的资本
我也曾悉数拥有
后来我努力活得像个人
却越来越不如一条狗
既不如宠物狗也不如流浪狗

Seen on the Seaside in Nan'ao

A wild black dog
By way of rape
Got on top of a wild white dog
The white dog half pushed, half gave in
And ran away, tail between her legs
After being thrust in three times
Looking like a scene (or a trick)
That we are familiar with
The black dog, his cock erected
Gave a wild chase
Till he held her in the grass
Giving her a wild fuck
I heard the gratification rolling
In the chest of the black dog
While the white dog repeated:
Don't stop! Don't stop!
I bore witness to this process of pleasurizing
Between the black and the white on the seaside in Nan'ao
They were vastly different
From the pet dogs in the residential *xiaoqu*
Ones that were decent
Dignified and walked in leisurely steps
Practised in restraining their own sex
I was impressed more
With what I saw just now
Of their primitiveness, roughness and wild passion
I once owned all
Their fucking capital
Subsequently, though, as I tried to live like a normal person
I was increasingly less like a dog
Neither a pet dog nor a stray one

七月的心肠

离开我一手创办
且经营了18年
的公司
之前
我在带有Logo的大门口
平静地
拍了最后一张照片
手机日记里我写下
"我走了，你自己保重
江湖险恶，愿你好运"
电梯门打开的刹那
我感到自己
稍微刻意地
硬了硬心肠

女儿幼儿园毕业
将经历人生中
第一次离别
一个月前我就问太太
你说离园的那一天
她懂得难过吗
"当然懂啊，现在说起
眼睛都是红红的"
幼儿园的最后一天
我和全家人一起去接她
看她依依不舍地
和小朋友道别
和老师说再见
她鼻子多酸我就多酸
她眼睛多红我就多红
她如果流泪我也无所谓哭出声来

Heart in July

Before I left
The company I had created
And been running
For 18 years
I stood outside the gate with the logo
And quietly
Shot the final photo
As I wrote an entry in my mobile phone diary
'I'm leaving. You take care of yourself
Rivers and lakes are a dangerous place. Good luck to you'
The instant the lift opened its doors
I felt that I myself
Had slightly hardened my heart
On purpose

Having graduated from the kindergarten
My daughter would have to experience the first farewell
In her life
A month earlier, I had asked my wife:
Would she know how to feel miserable
On the day when she left the kinder?
'Of course she does. Even when she mentioned it
Her eyes reddened'
The last day in the kinder
My whole family turned out to meet her
When I saw how reluctant she was
In saying goodbye to the other kids
And in taking farewell from her teachers
She choked up as I did
Her eyes reddened as my eyes did
And if she wept, I would weep, too

依旧是半个月前的那副心肠
但此刻自然松弛
或者说此一副的柔软，足以
晾制成鞭子
将彼一副的坚硬，反复抽打
令一个隐忍克制的老板
一个放任恣肆的父亲
同时现形

My heart remains where it was half a month ago
At the moment, though, it feels relaxed
Or, put another way, its softness now can be
Turned into a whip
To whip, repeatedly, the hardness of then
Making it possible for a boss with restraint
And an unrestrained father
To appear at the same time

谁和谁睡

起先A睡了B
一对甜蜜的恋人儿
分手若干年后
A和C一起睡了B
半年后C又单独睡了B
（睡之前他们按下免提
给A打了个电话）
现在ABC呆在
宾馆的双床房里
谁和谁睡
成为一个问题
后来他们穿过
摇摇晃晃的大堂
镜头里只剩
两张一米二的小床
略微揉皱的白床单
看上去非常失落
天空广大啊但床笫间的苦恼
一点儿也没有减少

Who is Sleeping with Whom

First, it was A who slept with B
A sweet couple
A few years after they split up
A and C, together, slept with B
Six months after, C slept alone with B
(before sleeping they pressed 'Hands-free'
And called A)
Right now, A, B and C are staying
In the double-bed room of a hotel
Who is going to sleep with whom
Has become an issue
Afterwards, when they went through
The shaking hall
What was left in the lens
Was two small beds, each 1.2 metre in length
With slightly crumpled white sheets
Looking very lost
The skies are vast but the vexation between beds
Has never been less

Five Poems about America: A Sequence

只关尊严

格里菲斯天文台
和盖蒂艺术中心
都是牛逼的地方
而且都不要钱
天文望远镜，随便看
梵高的名画，无任何防护
随便拍
两者有一个共同之处
——都是由私人捐建
但航母不是（也不该）
因此我猜航母会收门票
（如果它不收就是它的错）
而史蒂文森牧场的羊圈
肯定是要钱的
我和太太兴高采烈地
签下850刀
为了那几英尺的地契
和几条羊毛的尊严

Only Related to Dignity

Griffith Observatory
And Getty Arts Center
Are places of *niubi* or cow pushy
And nothing is charged for admission
You can freely watch through the telescope
And there's no protection around paintings by Van Gogh
Both with one thing in common:
They are private donations
Although the aircraft carrier isn't (or should be)
Hence my guess that they'll charge for admission
(If they don't that will be a mistake)
As for the sheep pen on Stevenson Ranch
They definitely will charge for admission
Excitedly, my wife and I
Signed the contract for 850 dollars
A title deed for the size of several feet
And the dignity for several sheets of wool

太平洋有时很大有时很小

领袖说太平洋够大
足以容得下某国和某国

但在我的飞行地图上
太平洋只容得下一架飞机

机头已到旧金山机屁股
还在上海

后来我在旧金山的酒店浏览境外网站
下意识地，竖起耳朵听着门外的动静

直到太太提醒，这里翻墙不犯法
我才睡了五年来的第一个安稳觉

The Pacific Ocean, Sometimes Big, Sometimes Small

The leader says that the Pacific Ocean is big enough
To contain a certain country and another certain country

But on my flight map
The Pacific Ocean can only contain an airplane

Its head having reached San Francisco
And its tail still in Shanghai

Later, when I was checking into websites outside China in a San Francisco hotel
I, subconsciously, erected my ears and listened for any movements outside the door

Till my wife reminded me that it was not illegal to climb the wall here
And that's when I had my first peaceful sleep in five years

偏见或肉体的种族主义

一群光屁股姑娘在台上跳舞
丁字裤，上半身裸
大部分白人，少部分黑人
我一点也不觉得美
更没有任何肉欲之念

光屁股的姑娘
我只喜欢黄种人
准确说只限东亚三国
这深处的偏见来自何处
但似乎不该由我道歉

Prejudice or Carnal Racism

A group of girls, naked bums, dancing on the stage
G-string, naked upper bodies
Mostly white audience, a small number of blacks
I didn't find anything beautiful about them
Nor did I have any carnal desire

Of the bare bum girls
I only love the yellow ones
To be more exact, the ones limited to the three countries in East Asia
Where does this in-depth prejudice come from?
But I don't seem to be the one to have to apologize

欢乐记

球场是欢乐的球
是欢乐的
球员是欢乐的观众是
欢乐的跳舞女郎的肤色
是欢乐的啊那每一寸
皮肤都流淌着自由
扣篮是欢乐的
盖帽是欢乐的
詹姆斯的激情是欢乐的
（可惜他不欢乐的时候就是个傻逼）
观众席上科比的羞涩是欢乐的
啊这家伙提前五分钟就走了
没有一个人找他签名
呐喊是欢乐的两次呐喊之间
短暂的寂静是欢乐的
刚入夜的城市是欢乐的
等待节日降临的国家是欢乐的
商场里买球衣的是欢乐的
户外吃汉堡的也是欢乐的
这就是他们的日常
他们的日常就是欢乐
让来自东方的诗人
被这原生的欢乐所感染
啊我为什么三十年没感到欢乐
（偶尔的欢乐也只在苟活和恐惧间偷得）
但一想到这个国家只负责欢乐
另一个国家只负责生产
想到那么多核弹和生化武器
正死死瞄准这个国家
我看到的欢乐似乎就没那么欢乐了
我也就回到我的日常我的日常
就只有他妈的悲伤

An Account of Joy

The playground is joyful the ball
Is joyful
The ballplayers are joyful the audience are
Joyful the colour of the dancing girls
Is joyful oh every inch
Of their skin is flowing with freedom
The dunking is joyful
The block shot is joyful
James' passion is joyful
(Pity he is a fool when he is not joyful)
The shyness of Kobe in the audience is joyful
Ah, this guy left five minutes ahead of time
No one sought his signature
Loud shouts are joyful the short quiet between the
Loud shouts is joyful
The city that has just entered into the night is joyful
The nation that is awaiting the descent of a festival is joyful
The one who buys a jersey in a shop is joyful
Those who eat hamburgers outdoors are joyful, too
That's their ordinary dailiness
Their ordinary dailiness is joyful
And affects the poet from the East
With this original joy
Ah, why did I never feel joy in my thirty years
(occasional joy stolen only out of an ignoble existence and fears)
But as soon as I thought of this country responsible for joy alone
And the other country only responsible for production
As well as the fact that so many atomic bombs and chemical weapons
Are dead on target at this country
The joy I saw did not seem to be so joyful
And I returned to my ordinary dailiness, ordinary dailiness
And all I've got is fucking sadness

我甚至想亲吻你鞋帮子上的雪花

在故国死了八回的
小肥羊火锅
在美国加州得以幸存
我来的是旧金山美臣街这家
船底木制成的后楼梯
不再听到偷渡者的叹息
啊祖国实在是太快了
被抛下的人民或侨民
仿佛都聚在这间餐馆里
慢吞吞地脱衣，点菜
（反正赶不上了）
想起多年前
深圳八卦岭小肥羊的店长
我太太的第一任房客
公司关门前请我们吃了最后一餐
然后赶着换了
三任女友，六份工作
祖国实在是太快了
但我宁愿慢一些
文火，慢炖
点好的菜死不上来
我们不急不躁地注视着窗外
被电车电线切割后的天空
冷峻，阴沉
仿佛在酝酿今冬的第一场雪
约翰半蹲着，开始检查壁炉
（第六代华工后人，刚从斯坦福毕业）
我则听到你在1987年冬天跺脚的声音

I Would Go So Far As to Kiss the Snowflakes on the Sides of Your Shoe

The little fat sheep hot pot
That had died eight times back in my own country
Has somehow survived in California, USA
I came to the one in Mason Street in San Francisco
On the back staircase, made of the bottom wood of a boat
I no longer heard the sighings of a stowaway
Ah, Motherland is so fast
That all the abandonees or émigrés
Seem to have gathered in this restaurant
As they, slowly, take off their clothes and order their food
(They can't catch up anyway)
I thought of how many years ago
Head of Little Fat Sheep at Bagualing, Shenzhen
And the first tenant of my wife's
Invited us to the last dinner before his company closed
Then, in a hurry, he
Changed three partners and six jobs
Motherland is so fast
Although I prefer to be slower
Slow fire, slow stewing
Our ordered food took ages to come
Patiently, we looked out the window
At the skies cut by the tram wires
Austere, gloomy
As if brewing the first snow this winter
John, half squatting, began to examine the furnace
(A sixth-generation Chinese, who has just graduated from Stanford)
I, though, heard your stampings in the winter of 1987

这一现象值得玩味

多年前一个国庆
（中国的国庆）
我在悉尼遇到一群澳籍华人
他们守在电视机前
通过卫星收看广场上的阅兵式
"太震撼了，看到祖国日益强大
我们海外华人也觉得扬眉吐气"
几年前另一个国庆
德国慕尼黑
我再次遇到一群德国籍华人
情况完全同上
眼神里同样看不出
失落和自卑
这些逃出来的中国人
移民前对党或政府
对这个国家，颇有微词
甚至敌意
但一旦成为侨民
对万里之外的祖国
反而爱得十分纯粹
（老吴说他们把乡愁误以为爱，老赵说
当伤害鞭长莫及反而更想装得像个人）
因此我能否认为
那些想移民的人
都是为了在万里之外
重新指认一个祖国
就像鹰，鹰的故乡是
岩石上闪电的伤痕
但它一次次迎着暴风起飞
拥抱那死亡和霹雳统御的长空

Something Worth Pondering

On National Day many years ago
(Chinese National Day)
We met a group of Chinese Australians in Sydney
They were waiting around television
And watching the parade on the Square via satellite
'So amazing to see Motherland becoming daily powerful
And we overseas Chinese are feeling uplifted'
On another National Day a few years ago
In Munich, Germany
I ran into a group of Chinese Germans
Same thing happened
You couldn't see from their eyes
Loss or low self-esteem
These Chinese escapees
Before they migrated
Were quite critical of the Party or the government
And of the country, and were even
Hostile to them
However, as soon as they became the residents in a foreign country
Their love became pure
Of Motherland tens of thousands of kilometres away
(According to Old Zhao, this is nostalgia mistaken as love, and he said
When hurt is too far to hurt, one, on the contrary, pretends to be more man than man)
For this reason, I wonder
If those who want to migrate
Do so in order to newly designate
A motherland tens of thousands of kilometres away
Like eagles whose hometown is
The scars of lightning on the rock
Although they, again and again, always fly against the storm
To embrace the long skies reigned by death and thunderbolts

高原之上

我偶尔会怀念故乡的陕北高原
怀念那里原生态的几千座大山
那里的每一座山都可以登顶
极目远眺，世界秩序分明
有人喜欢爬上山顶喊几嗓子
倾听山谷间的回声
胸中块垒一泻千里
而在我多年客居的南方丘陵
每一座山都被荆棘覆盖
它是蛇和蜥蜴的天堂
但不适合人类攀爬
因此总令人压抑，难以释怀
我最容易在秋天的夜晚想起故乡
当然令我心驰神往的
不仅仅是高原
还有高原之上
别的一些什么

On the Plateau

Occasionally, I miss the Northern Shaanxi Plateau, my hometown
The thousands of mountains of original ecology there
The top of every one of them I can ascend to
Where I can see as far as the eye can see and where the world order is clear
Some like to come to the top of the mountain and give a few shouts
To listen to the echoes in the valleys
And shed all the shit accumulated in the heart for miles
While every one of the southern hills where I lived like a guest for years
Was covered by thorns
A paradise for snakes and lizards
Not fit for human beings to climb
Hence a depression that one finds hard to get over
It's so easy for me to think of my hometown on nights of autumn
But, of course, what fascinates me
Is not just the plateau
But something else
On it

和儿子捉迷藏

天色几分钟就暗下来了
速度远超我的想象
这是游戏的第三轮
前两轮有些乏味，躲在临近的
柱子后面，甚至故意弄出些响动
这一次我准备躲到
他翻不过来的小区墙外
暮色四合掩盖几百米外的高铁站
他再也找不到爸爸
（他总有彻底找不到我的一天）
像被质押的爱国者，被动失去他
流放的祖国
我捂紧口罩，克制住焦虑
坚持不暴露自己
等他带有哭腔的呐喊再大声些

Playing Hide-and-Seek with My Son

The sky darkened soon enough, in a few minutes
At a speed faster than I had imagined
It's now the third round of the game
The first two a bit boring, hiding myself behind
A nearby column, and even making noise on purpose
This time, I'm going to hide myself
Behind the wall of *xiaoqu* that he can't climb over
When darkness falls and conceals the high-speed rail station hundred metres away
He won't find his dad again
(There will be a day when he won't ever find me again)
Like a pledged patriot, forced to lose his
Exiled country
I held tight my mask, trying not to be too anxious
Not to reveal myself
Waiting for his tearful cries to get louder

策略和语言

两个大国
干架
死伤四五十人
这在我和加勒万河谷看来
都是个庞大的数字

两个核大国
干架
不用枪炮
只用木棒和石块
就互相弄死几十人

开枪打死几十人
用木棒和石块砸死几十人
哪个更令你惊讶，哪个
更接近残忍，或者
更远离文明

但至少构成语言的成功
现在我只能说
某国和某国，干了一架
而不能说它们打了一仗
更不能说发生了一场战争

Strategy and Language

The big powers
Were fighting
Forty to fifty people died or got wounded
Which is a huge number
To me or the Galwan River Valley

The two nuclear powers
Were fighting
Not with guns or cannons
But with sticks and stones
And that has led to scores of deaths

Which one is more surprising
Shooting scores dead or
Smashing scores dead with sticks and stones, or which
Is closer to cruelties or
Further away from civilization

At least, it has achieved the success of language
All I can say now
Is that a country has had a fight with another
But I can't say that they have fought a battle
Least of all can I say a war has taken place

地球是一只睾丸观念是另一只

安全套是最被滥用的
政治正确，越来越薄
（越声称恍若无物就越证实其有）
润滑油的人道关怀，难掩
睾丸上粗鄙的利己主义
现在它被一条
大金链子牵着，主人必须
胖，横肉，系山寨爱马仕皮带
夫人们谈论的精致
从来都是一场误会。天生缺乏
教养，耐心，和基本的良善
注定只能流于粗鄙
至于原则和美德
只是皮带中间那个锈死的卡扣
张大龙问你是否在影射那位
以足球献的豫籍地产商
事实上我只想腹诽一番中医
作为左派中最铁杆的盟友
傻逼硅谷始终想活埋华尔街
但杂种华尔街
只不过想买到来自硅谷的潮货
参加一次蒙面派对

The Earth is One Testicle and Concept is the Other

Condoms, being the most abused
Political correctness, have now become thinner and thinner
(the more they claim they don't seem to exist the more they prove they do)
Lubricant's humanitarian concern finds it hard to conceal
The rude egoism of the testicles
As they are now being led
By a big gold chain, their master must
Be fat, beefy, and have a fake Hermes belt
While the exquisiteness the wives talk about
Is always a mistake. A naturally born lack
Of upbringing, patience and basic kindness
Is bound to lead to vulgarity
As for principles and virtues
They are the rusty belt buckle that got stuck
Zhang Dalong said: Are you referring to
The property developer from Henan who donated with soccer
In fact I was only meaning to slander the traditional Chinese doctor in my belly
A most die-hard ally among the leftists
The stupid Silicon Valley has always wanted to bury Wall Street alive
But all the bastard Wall Street ever wants
Is to purchase new stuff from Silicon Valley
In order to attend a masquerade ball

打补丁的方法论

整个小学时代我只有一条
蓝色的劳动布裤子
有一天右边膝盖
破了一个洞
煤油灯下母亲连夜给它
打了一个补丁
反而遭到同学们的讪笑
姑妈的建议是别打补丁
把洞撕大，要比
所有同学的破洞都大
最好露出鸡鸡，和
鸡鸡上的纹身
父亲的意见则是
在左右两个膝盖
各打一个补丁
（对不起啊左膝盖）
现在土地尚未分配
他们就为选谁当总统争论不休
但我倾向于姑妈
她有望统治全人类的躁暴美学
完胜我爸的北欧社会主义

The Patched-up Methodology

In all my primary school years, I had only
One pair of blue labour-cloth trousers
One day, a hole appeared
On the right knee
By the kerosene light, Mother worked overnight
Patching it up
Which was ridiculed by my classmates
My paternal aunty recommended not patching it up
But tearing the hole up so that it was bigger
Than all their holes
Better still if my dick was exposed, along
With the tattoo on it as well
Father was of the opinion that there ought to be a patch
On either the left or the right knee
(Sorry, my left knee)
Even before the land was undivided
They had already started arguing about who should be elected the president
But I was inclined towards my aunty
A likely candidate to reign over mankind's violent aesthetics
And my father's socialism of a northern European variety

那个说谎的人又得了一枚勋章

我站在星期五傍晚的一棵树下
耐心地等车
半个月前跳起来才能
够得着的枝条
此刻正轻拍我的脸
是谁赐予它向下的力量
为何要借助一米七四的我
与大地的疼痛相连
触摸那忧虑深深的额头
一阵电流通过我，像麻木穿过
树桩的每一条纤维
我闭上眼睛，和它一起感受
亚细亚大陆，正牵起欧亚板块
加速坠入地狱之火
在那里它将有所作为
将病毒涂满异见者的脸
你瞧那个说谎的人又得了一枚勋章
25g，足以锁住一万只乌鸦的舌头

The Liar Has Won Another Medal

Standing under a tree of a Friday evening
I was patiently waiting for the bus
The branches I would have had to jump
To reach half a month ago
Were gently patting me on the face
But who gave them the downward force
To connect with the pain of the land
Via the 1.74-metre length of me
When they touched my head of deep worries
There was a sensation of electrical current going through me, like numbness that
Penetrated every nerve of a tree stump
I closed my eyes to feel along with them
How Asia Minor was connecting with the Eurasian Plate
To speed up the fire that was falling into hell
Where it would make a difference
By smearing the virus all over the faces of the dissidents
Look, the liar has won another medal
Its 25 grams sufficient to lock up the tongues of 10,000 magpies

牛肉面馆的黄昏

暮色流入一碗牛肉拉面
让吞吸者的表情
突然有些悲滞
尽管他已经努力掩饰了
黑头巾的老板娘
注视着锈蚀的玻璃门
笨重地开合
像一根鱼刺卡在下午
和南山之间
一种习得性无助
念及我退守回乡的朋友
连续几个月
他都在黔西南一条
陌生的河上钓鱼
（我从没问过他的收成）
幸亏失控坠落的反舰导弹
只是压扁一枚啤酒瓶盖
许久之后我们依旧听到它
砰砰滚动的声音

Evening in the Beef Noodle Restaurant

Colours of the evening were flowing into a bowl of beef ramen
So much so that the sucking and swallowing guy
Looked somewhat sad
Even though he had tried to look otherwise
The woman boss, in a black scarf
Was watching the rusty glass door
Open and close, heavily
Like a fishbone stuck between the afternoon
And the Nanshan Hill
With an acquired sense of helplessness
I missed my friend who had retreated to his home village
And for months after
He went fishing on a strange river
In the southwestern Guizhou
(I never ask how much he has got)
Fortunately, an anti-ship missile that fell after it had lost control
Managed to only squash a beer bottle cap
Long after that, we can still hear its
Rolling sound

困顿山小记

十月的一个下午
我独自登上困顿山北坡的一条小路
秋天正向纵深处推进，局部
已经留出了雪的位置
（几只乌鸦蹲在雪上的位置）
四寂无人，只有
百鸟鸣呖
在它们自由繁荣的家园
完全无视一个陌生的闯入者
我已从人类的名利场中
完败归来
无意重入鸟的阵营
即使它们
降调合唱一支迎宾曲
指挥群山舞起黑白琴键
我也只是来此虚度一番
天黑之前就会离开

An Account of Mount Exhaustion

On one afternoon in October
I went alone up the northern slope of Mount Exhaustion along a path
The autumn was pushing into the depths, part of it
Already reserving space for the snow
(several magpies were squatting on the snow positions)
No one seen, just
Hundreds of birds singing
Paying no attention to a total stranger, a trespasser
In their free and prosperous garden
I have returned from the vanity fair of the world
A total failure
With no intention to rejoin the birds
Even if they lower their tones to sing a welcome tune
To direct the mountains to dance their black and white keys
I came here just to waste my time for a while
And would soon leave before dark

203路公共汽车

陌生女子，二十四、五岁
模样中等，穿职业套裙
此刻倚窗而立，将吊环抓得紧紧
吸引我的并不是这些
而是她的膝盖
两只膝盖，上面密密布有
竹凉席的印记
长方形，口香糖般大小
仿佛生活在身体上盖了些章
这是1996年十分流行的
一种竹凉席，大街小巷叫卖声声
我已经猜到她是公司白领
租房子，和男友同居
房间没有冷气
喜欢在这些湿津津的夜晚
双膝跪地，将汗水洗过的白屁股
高高翘起来
当晚回家我就和女友
模拟了一把
第一次采取这狗爬式
足足折腾了一个小时
膝盖上的印记，果然
如出一辙
此后每天专坐203路
但再也没见过那个
无比性感的女子

Bus 203

An unfamiliar woman, 24 or 25 years of age
Medium looks, in a professional suit dress
Was now leaning against the window, taking a tight grip of the strap overhead
What attracted me was not that
But her knees
That were covered, thickly
With the print marks of a cool bamboo mat
Each mark oblong, the size of a chewing gum
Like seals put on her body by life
It was the kind of bamboo mat that was popular
In 1996 when you could hear peddlers crying their wares from street to street
I could guess she's a white collar in a company
Renting, living with her boyfriend
No aircon in her room
Who loved spending the sweaty nights
On her knees, raising her white buttocks, washed with her sweat
In the air
When I returned home that night, my girlfriend and I
Gave it a go by imitating the girl
Adopting the doggy style, for the first time
For a full hour
The print marks on her knees, sure enough
Were exactly the same
Afterwards, I would choose to go by Bus 203 every day
But had never met that
Infinitely sexy girl again

跨省客车

从暮色中开出的跨省客车
带着我的悲伤
这个城市有七个长途汽车站
但我只有同一种悲伤
仿佛它带走我所有的
朋友，情人和情敌
这个省份有四个邻省
这个国家有十几个邻国
但我只有同一个情敌
事实上客车开往哪里
车上坐着什么人
和我有什么关系
和我的悲伤又有什么关系
事实上我认识的人
逃离本城时
都选择飞机或火车
我一点都不难过，完全麻木
但这些大客车，这些黄昏
尤其雨前沉闷的黄昏
乌云低低地抚摸它的额头
一些不知名的鸟儿在顶上盘旋
这时，只要这些钢铁家伙闷一声启动
我的悲伤就无以复加
有一回我尾随几辆，走出几十公里
终于看清车上没有一个乘客
它们空空如也驶离本城，只载着
我的悲伤，只为将我的悲伤
运抵郊外，雪一样披挂在肃穆的旷野上

On the Interprovincial Coach

The interprovincial coach that started in motion in the colours of the evening
Carried my sadness
This city has seven long-distance coach stations
But all I have is one variety of sadness
As if it took away all
My friends, mistresses and enemies
This province has four adjacent provinces
This country has more than a dozen adjacent countries
But all I have is one enemy
In fact it has got nothing to do with me
Or with my sadness
Wherever the coach is going
And whoever is sitting in it
In fact, when people I know
Left the city
They chose to go by air or train
I didn't feel awful, I was completely numb
But these coaches, these evenings
Particularly the kind that was gloomy before rain
The dark clouds lowered themselves to touch their foreheads
While nameless birds were circling around their tops
Right now, whenever these steely things got started with a booming noise
My sadness would become infinite
On one occasion, I tailgated a number of them for scores of kilometers
But all I managed to see was there was not a single passenger
They left the city empty, carrying my sadness
Only, for the purpose of carrying my sadness
To the outskirts of the city, to spread it over the solemn wilderness, like snow